MYTHOLOGY OF MY BONES

Linda M. Crate

<u>Dedication</u>

I dedicate this book to anyone who is struggling with their identity or sexuality. You are valid, you matter, and you are loved.

Foreword

I was hesitant about putting this book out into the world, at first, but as I kept seeing hateful and cruel comments towards the lgbtq+ community, I felt that it were a necessary step.

I know I might get some hate or disapproval for this, but I am done hiding my true identity.

I feel that it's important everyone feels comfortable in their own skin. Some people might consider this "lifestyle" a sin, but no one really has a choice in who they love. I think it's absurd they have any right to judge anyone especially because their own book (if we're going by the bible) instructs them to do everything in love and that God is love and we're all made in the image of God.

So if that is true then everyone regardless of their race, gender, sexuality, etc. is made in God's image making us all equal in his eyes, meaning that we are all deserving and worthy of love. I refuse to believe that any of these people judging truly understand that all some of us are trying to do is live our lives as who we are without getting judgment, hatred, or being targeted and murdered simply because we are different from other people.

This isn't me trying to cause a scene or make myself special. I have always been beautiful and unique in my own way, and my worth doesn't cease or decrease because of my sexual identity. I think the world with all its vibrancy and variations is beautiful, as it is, and there's no reason to hate someone just because you don't understand them. It doesn't make you right and them wrong.

If we can agree to disagree and work through our differences like normal people, that's great. But I am sick of the bullying, the name calling, and the rudeness of people with differing views. I understand that not everyone thinks of lgbtq+ as something valid, but we exist and we are worthy of respect regardless of how one may feel.

I am tired of people trying to make me feel inadequate in some way because I am not straight. This book is a direct result of that.

Acknowledgments

would you cease to love me was first published in pixel heart magazine.

japanese flowers was first published in Anti-Heroin Chic.

Contents

kindred spirits

you don't get to choose your sexuality, just as you don't choose
your name or the color of your eyes or if you have a mental
illness; i think a part of me always knew—but when it was
famous women i had crushes on, it was easier to ignore, it wasn't
as if i would ever come across them on the streets in rural
pennsylvania; i could just say i found them pretty without judgment
or condemnation—growing up in the church i knew a woman's
place was meant to be with a man, and i did always care for
them, too; but in college i met someone i could not deny i felt a
pull toward—another woman, a friend, and when the realization
dawned on me i was a mess of emotions tangled and jumbled and
confused; i feared my family would reject me so i buried this
secret deep inside of me and remained behind a locked closet
door—but i am done hiding, done pretending, done hating myself; i
am who i am and i love who i love—i will never be ashamed that
my heart sees kindred spirits and doesn't worry about the rest.
-linda m. crate

i will take pride in who i am

love is love
no longer am i
ashamed,
won't stand in the shadows;
i won't condemn myself
because plenty of people would do that
for me—
i won't pretend this closet can hold me,
or that skeletons are good
conversationalists;
i won't pretend that i didn't love her—
but i am sorry
if that brings shame to anyone i love
i am sorry that i couldn't be what you needed
me to be,
but i refuse to be ashamed of myself;
my heart has always been full of light and love
and rainbows have always been my favorite
i will take pride in who i am
even if you cannot.
-linda m. crate

would you cease to love me?

"you better not
be a lesbian"
i'm not,
but once i loved
a girl
who can only be
best described by the hue
of pink;
i find her in roses
and sunsets
in anime and in girls
who have pink hair as she
once did—
i find her in whispers
of my memory,
and in the songs of our
mutual friends;
she no longer speaks to me
over a misunderstanding
because i wounded her in a way
she could not forgive—
i still remember
she always smelled of roses,
and she woke in me
the dreaming when i thought it was dead;
she taught me our scars make
us beautiful and unique
because of her i can remember my voice
and speak as i was always meant to—

you saw a strange soul
i saw a kindred one,
and if i were a lesbian;
would i not still be your daughter
or would you cease to love me?
- linda m. crate

we don't have to answer to each other

all my life
i was taught
that it was wrong
for a woman to love
another woman
or a man to love another man
so when i couldn't deny
the fact i had fallen
for one of my friends i was
thrown for a loop,
confusion and anger forged
a hot path through me;
i feared judgment and i feared God
all i wanted was to become invisible
seep through the floorboards
ceased to exist—
i thought my brain was going to explode
didn't know how to process this,
prayed for a cure that never came;
i still love her to this very day and i have since
realized that God is love and love is love
so live and let live because we don't have to
answer to each other—
our lives are our own to forge.
-linda m. crate

she woke in me the dreaming

i think a part of me always knew,
but i denied;
hid my crushes in hollywood
where none of them
could find me—
there were girls i found pretty,
but i admired them for their strength and character;
saw them as nothing more than
friends—
it wasn't until college i fell in love with a girl
different than anyone i knew before
she shook loose dust
from me,
reminded me of my power and my dreams;
awoke my consciousness
from a frail and broken existence into reality
reminding me that i did matter and so did my dreams—
she woke in me the dreaming
when i thought it were dead within me,
and i will never be able to thank her enough for freeing
myself from the bondage
of being trapped in nightmares.
-linda m. crate

japanese flowers

the only woman i loved as something other than friend was also
the one who taught me that my scars made me beautiful—she
looked at my scars after my gallbladder surgery and said they
looked like japanese flowers as she traced over the scar with her
fingers, and she told me that she couldn't understand my shame
because she found our scars made us beautiful; it turns out she
was right—in every broken place that's where the light always
gets in me—she always struck me as otherworldly; a faerie that
smelled of roses who was both vulnerable and soft yet fierce and
thorned—she reawakened dreams in me when i thought the
dreaming was dead, and accepted me as i was; all these years
and years later after the misunderstanding that unraveled our
friendship, i still find her unforgettable—my grandmother said she
was a bit of a character, but i think that was why i loved her so
much.

-linda m. crate

let your rainbow shine bright

i will never fathom
why some people will never
be proud of their children,
why they will never
support their pride;
i don't understand those
who claim to love yet cannot love
their children because of their
sexual orientation—
no one should have to live
in the closet,
disguising who they are
simply to appease society;
i will never truly comprehend why
some people have to be made to feel
they have no right to exist
when there are bigots that insist
they're entitled to existence—
if your parents cannot support you
know that there are others that do
be proud of who you are
let your rainbow shine bright.
-linda m. crate

creating a better world

in a world that's plastic
a brave act
is simply being yourself,
but i will have pride
in who i am;
because i am full of love
in a world full of hate—
full of light
in a world that too often
knows darkness,
and i am not ashamed
of who i am regardless of what others
may say or think of me;
because my path isn't theirs to walk
just as theirs is not mine—
my identity is my own,
and i will sing my song
because i have no other psalm
i can claim for myself;
and even if i did
i wouldn't
because we each must be who we are—
we have no choice but to be ourselves,
and i won't comform to the way of this world
when i know there's a better one i am
meant to help create.
-linda m. crate

i will embrace who i am

"you better not be a lesbian"
those words still haunt me,
i'm not;
just happened to love a girl before
i am not ashamed anymore—
at the time my brain nearly exploded
didn't know how to feel,
confusion and rage washed over me
in equal measured waves;
and i never told my family because
i was so scared of their rejection—
but i am who i am
won't hide my truth to make others
comfortable,
love is love;
and it is the only magic we have in this world
which has the power to save us all
so i will embrace who i am regardless of who
cannot stand my pride—
because my heart and my life are my own to live,
and my path is my own to walk.
-linda m. crate

they were wrong

"we will support the girls, and whoever they
love. although we hope it's guys."
i always wonder about that, i know most people
don't want their daughters or sons to be
anything less than straight;
but what does it matter?
love is love.
people should be able to take pride in who they are
without fear of judgment or shame,
people should be able to be who they are
without being killed for it;
no one is inferior because of who they love
it's not as if anyone gets to decide
a heart falls for a heart, a soul connects to a soul
regardless of gender—
maybe one day people who think orientation
is a choice
will understand that it isn't when they fall for someone
"they're not supposed to",
and maybe instead of repressing it they will come
to the understanding they were wrong.
-linda m. crate

spells of love and light

wave that rainbow flag
proudly,
don't be ashamed of who you are;
there should be no shame
in love—
no one has the right to judge anyone,
and they shouldn't
even though they always do;
you just do you
because you have every right to exist
and have pride in who you are
even if they don't understand—
hold your head up even if there are others
committed to misunderstanding who
you are
because you have every right to exist,
to dream, to live, to hope, and to be;
just as much as anyone else does—
don't let anyone tell you who you are
or who to be because only you could know that,
and your destiny is your own to manifest;
so conjure your magic and send out
your spells of love and light
anyway you see fit.
-linda m. crate

my prayer

i see your hate and your condemnation, why do you think i've
stayed in the closet so long? but i am done being ashamed. i am
proud of who i am. my heart is a heart that loves, my soul is a soul
that is deep, and my intentions for others are always good; i am
not the monsters that have always sought to break me or the hells
every devil i've faced has given me—i am something stronger,
made of love and light; i am immortal of flame—daughter of the
sun and moon, i refuse to do anything less than shine; full of
dreams and hope i stand even when my faith in the universe
wavers—even when my lips quiver, and the tears spill; i always
rise from the ashes of my death and rise again—not everyone is
brave enough to stand once they have fallen, but i refuse to stay
on my knees; my prayer is that one day everyone will understand
the only choice we should make is love and not judgment—live
and let live, you don't get to decide who you love and neither does
anyone else.

-linda m. crate

a chance to bloom

you don't want us to exist
or give us room to grow,
you don't want us to admit
our truths or face the fact you
put us through evils;
you don't want to admit that your
daughters or your sons are less—
but i have never understood
what about the lgbtq+ community
makes a person less,
if anything we have more of a capacity
to love and to understand;
than all those who think to condemn us—
i understand the world can be a scary place
or there are things you don't understand,
but please recognize your anger is misplaced;
we just want acceptance of who we are
even if you can't understand you can love
without agenda or condition as family is meant to—
a flower doesn't bloom in mere darkness
it requires light
so don't choke us of our growth
just because you don't understand who we are,
we deserve a chance to bloom.
-linda m. crate

you'll never be my god

everyone wants to come for my light
either a parasite who wants to steal it
or a devil that wishes to break me,
but i refuse to be the monsters who hunt
me in the light of day and the darkness
of night;
i refuse to be all the beasts that tried
to break me—
i will use my lantern light
to burn away nightmares and devils
so that the path of goodness can be illuminated,
but i won't refuse to admit who i am
so you can be comfortable;
i won't water myself down or turn down
my frequency or intensity
you should be ashamed for asking me to be anyone else
but me—
i may not be straight,
but that doesn't mean there's no value in my bones
or in my life or in me;
and you don't get to tell me i don't matter because i know i do—
if i had no worth then you wouldn't try so hard to
shatter my power,
but you can't have it;
you'll never be my god.
-linda m. crate

restless fangs

you can't pray the gay away
trust me
i've tried,
but all that was taken from me
was my shame and my pain;
my confusion and my rage ebbed away
i realized that love was never wrong
just the way i had been taught—
it's our choices in life
that define who we are,
and i will always choose love;
no matter how many times i have been hurt
it is the only magic that can save us all—
the only salve that will save us
from the wicked nightmares and their restless fangs.
-linda m. crate

i will war if that is what you ask of me

i'm going to face the fire
won't burn in the flames because
i am a daughter of the moon
have oceans roaring at my beck and call,
and you may think you have the upper hand;
but i refuse to fall prey before those
who would demonize us—
just because my arrow is bent doesn't mean
it cannot do damage,
my heart prefers peace but i can battle
in a war if that is what you ask of me;
will make you bleed in places you didn't even know
existed—
i am done keeping my silence,
of being locked in the closet for your comfort;
you want to say that our politics is fascism?
i am just trying to live in this world,
just want to be loved and accepted for who i am;
there's nothing vile or despicable about that—
stop fearing what you don't know
because your hate and anger are making you
a fool.
-linda m. crate

bones of shame

i didn't want to admit who i was
for the longest time
because i lived in the bones of shame,
i am no longer afraid
even if it costs me friends or family
because i cannot help but be who i am;
i love a person because of their soul
not their gender
somehow it seems more pure
to me—
i know not everyone will understand,
but this my path and my journey;
it is my cross to carry
should you wish to abandon me it's okay
i am used to being left alone
when i need people the most
just remember i would never do the same
to you—
my sexuality doesn't define me
nor does it make me less than who i was or am or will be,
i have always been worth it and i always will be;
done playing pretend and make believe
with my life
sometimes i love people i am told i shouldn't.
-linda m. crate

sometimes your words hurt me

i remember when you said
"that's interesting"
in regards to *jenny's wedding*
then insisted that i better not be a lesbian
as if a person gets to choose
their sexuality,
and i couldn't gain hold of my voice;
usually you are kind and understanding
i am a person who loves without
condition
so i didn't grasp that there could be
this fault in you—
i love you,
but sometimes i wonder if telling my story
is the right thing;
will you still love me when you discover my truths?
or will you try to pray my identity away
until i am what you deem normal,
i love you and i always will;
but i cannot pretend that sometimes your words don't hurt me
just as mine sometimes wound you.
-linda m. crate

i'm dreaming somewhere beneath the rain-bow

i am always dreaming
there's always this underlying hope
i will help create a better world,
and i will sew shut generations
of wounds so that we can all breathe
a lot easier;
perhaps that is egotistical in your eyes
but i have kind intentions for myself and the people
in this world
my love will help cull the hate on this earth
because it is magic
it is a spell that snakes through every darkness
and destroys nightmares—
i am not afraid of who i am,
neither should you be;
my heart is full of light and love and i want everyone
to be able to enjoy life beneath the rainbow
no matter what reason they may hold it sacred—
i will take pride in who i am
even if no one else can
because my sexuality is for me and my love
not anyone else to know,
and in the end
i am who i am
regardless of who you may want me to be.
-linda m. crate

you're just a pharisee

you say doctrine matters yet you hold your banners of hatred and
anger high, if God is love then should you not echo it? He sent His
son to die for you because he loves you, but He also loves me and
her and him; and everyone else in this universe—it is not just
about you and your wants and needs, it is something much more
deep than that; we are all connected and we all matter—you
cannot make someone irrelevant just because they disagree with
your narrow minded point of view, you cannot throw enough
shade to make people go back into their closets; we are exhausted
of being held ransom for our sexuality—you love your rules a little
too much to be a person of God so let me call your bluff, i don't
believe you; take your rules and burn with them because you're
just a pharisee.
-linda m. crate

we can all be civil

why do you hate me? why are you so repulsed? my heart isn't
dirty like your hands, my soul isn't black as your hate; and yet you
would say i were the evil one—you would deny my goodness and
my virtue to fit your rhetoric, insist that i were not worthy of love;
because you cannot love a sinner although you have sinned—it is
not for you or anyone else to judge me, but you've made yourself
gods; you sit on imaginary thrones so you can kick me—why? all i
do is spill over with love, i love everyone unconditionally: friends,
family, lovers; with an intensity that can outshine even the sun—
all i ever wish for anyone is for them to achieve their happiness, i
just want to be treated with dignity and respect; i don't think that
is too much to ask—i know sometimes i speak in anger but have
you heard your voice? it isn't kind, it is dark and filthy like a dark
and stagnant river full of monsters hiding in the darkness ready to
devour; all i want is for you to understand even if we must agree
to disagree that we can all be civil—there is no need for calamity,
no reason for either of us to struggle; we can be kind to one
another and we can be friends even if we do not agree on every-
thing—i just cannot accept bigotry or condemnation and if you
insist upon using either of these tools to hold against my throat,
then we cannot be friends; i am not ashamed of who i am any-
more.

-linda m. crate

you hate me with a hate beyond hate

i guess it's easier to hate a person
to make them wrong, to insist they don't know
rather than confronting the ugliness
inside your own soul;
none of us is perfect yet you hate me
for something i cannot even control
i have had anxiety for as long as i can remember
bouts of depression, too—
i try to make everyone's life better because i know
what it is like to suffer
yet i feel rejected and alone when i read your words,
why do you get to hate me when all i want to do
is heal the world, to be accepted, to make the world
a better place for everyone?
i am sick of wearing these chains
of hiding beneath the fabric of scars
praying and hoping that you won't find out who i truly am
because i hate the idea of being rejected
so many have seen my love and walked away
despite the fact that i love without condition or asking anything in
return,
maybe i make it too easy;
all i know is that i love with a love beyond love and you hate me
with a hate beyond hate.
-linda m. crate

not of your world

red, orange, yellow, green, blue, indigo, violet
make up the colors of a rainbow
prism of light dancing through tears of water;
i made a rainbow in fifth grade using
water and plastic wrap—
i have always loved rainbows,
their beauty has always enchanted me;
every color like every person in the universe
with their own personalities and beauty
some more vibrant and some a little more shy
yet all equally as lovely—
it is a pity that you abandon every beautiful thing
of you to embrace the ugly parts opening
wounds in the hearts and souls of others because
they aren't who you would like them to be,
does it really matter who someone loves?
you act as if the whole world sees everything
through the lens of your eyes,
but i am grateful that we all have our own lenses;
i would hate to see things through your narrow minded
point of view
where you only deserve love if you are straight
as an arrow—
because only those who cling rigidly to rules
living in absolutes could be right,
after all might makes right in your world;
but i thank God it's not mine.
-linda m. crate

i regret nothing

it is easier just to hide who i am from you, but i could never be content; skeletons make poor conversationalists—i want to be more than just bare bones walking around as a shell of who i am, and for so long i have been hiding who i am out of fear and out of shame; but i am ready to discard both like shed skin—i am rising from the ashes of who i once was to burn brighter than i ever have, immortal of the flame, i am the phoenix rising always every time i die; it isn't always the easiest thing to do but it is always worth it—once i loved a girl, and i love her still; i won't be embarrassed of that anymore—it may not be normal, but i have never found joy in the mundane, anyway; i have always been told i am weird so let me dance to the beat of my own drummer—i promise i am happier being me than i ever would be being anyone else, no one else has my voice or my heart; no one has my lens or my soul—and no one can dance just the way i do and i regret nothing.
-linda m. crate

rules aren't more important than people

you think you can hold my head beneath the water? i am the
moon's daughter, i will only reverse the curse of death upon you
instead; i prefer kindness and compassion because i have a heart
full of wildflowers and butterflies but i can also be a villain should
the story call for one—so many want to vilify me for my gender,
anyway; so i guess the fact that i loved another woman before
makes me disgusting in their eyes—i don't care what they believe,
i know i have a heart full of love and light; i know that there is
beauty in rainbows and they're for everyone regardless of the
fact that some would stake a claim and insist it only belongs to
them—if doctrine is more important to you than loving people
perhaps you're practicing your religion wrong because love is the
only power we have to change the world, the only magic that will
decimate hatred; i refuse to believe that rules are more imporant
than people.
-linda m. crate

and i will not listen

you are like wasps
trying to sting me
simply because i exist

must mean i have some
power that you fear,
but i won't give up that power

simply so you can strike
me down;
i will not stop being me

because you want me watered down
since you cannot make sense of me
otherwise—

i will not be drowned in your nightmares
won't collect your inheritance of hatred
you aren't my parents

just people who tell me how i should
live my life without knowing me or my path,
and i will not listen;

i have always been stubborn
just ask my parents
i know who i am and i don't care what people think.
-linda m. crate

you were the villain

you carve wounds with your words,
but you don't care;
you want everyone to know you're a king
strong and ruthless
your words are final—
go ahead and give me your thunder storms
i have always loved the scent after the rain,
washes away my pain;
i won't be overthrown in my own kingdom
won't ever be your queen
because i am the king of this kingdom—
you say i am wrong because once i loved a woman,
i say you're wrong because you don't know
how to love;
sometimes society can be cruel but it doesn't mean
that i will let them or you bite me
i am not someone you can devour—
got claws and fangs of my own
so go ahead and provoke
the outcast,
i promise it will end in blood;
and you probably won't like your part in the novel
when it's revealed that *you* were the villain not me.
-linda m. crate

heart full of love

piece by piece
you pick at me
not intentionally,
of course,
but your posts are
deliberately
baiting and cruel
to people like me;
people who stand outside
the status quo
people who have always
been outcasts—
my love may be intense and deep,
but i know that is not why
you'd shun it;
it's because i have the capacity
to love any soul who is on the same
wavelength as mine—
remove my heart and you will find
i have love even for you,
you who would hate me;
just for existing.
-linda m. crate

i am not weak

you expect vulnerability out of me,
and i'll admit i do feel everything
in a wide spectrum of emotions that i
couldn't adequately use words
to explain;
but don't think i will throw myself
at your feet
begging for your approval
i won't—
years ago i learned my power and i took it back
reclaimed my voice and my magic,
and i refuse to be locked in any cage where
i need someone's approval to survive;
love me for who i am and all that i am
or watch me walk out the door
i am done living in shame and in agony
to satiate your need—
i may be sensitive,
but i am not weak.
-linda m. crate

you're lacking

i will not argue with you,
won't try to convince you i am right;
but i will defend my right to exist

you say something about straight parades
be thankful you don't need one
that you can exist in a safe place without fear

of insult, injury, or death
simply because you are alive;
i don't know why you cannot see

people are suffering not because of
a sexuality they couldn't choose but because
people being cruel and vicious and no one is doing

anything to stop it even saying
they deserve it—
but does anyone really deserve to suffer?

it is not something i would wish upon anyone
simply for existing
perhaps some compassion and empathy

you would find you're lacking in
perhaps you would find if you looked in your life people
who love with a love purer than yours.
-linda m. crate

i have a lot of anger

i guess you think a decline in acceptance
would be a good thing
considering you only accept what you want
to believe as truth?
i guess it would be better for me
to hate myself and be ashamed of who i am
simply lock me in a closet and forget about me
because you are about as cuddly as a cactus
and every bit of prickly with your speech
if you are to speak the truth in love
with compassion and understanding
maybe people would listen,
but i refuse to listen to someone who insists
lgbt+ people are political fascists;
someone who thinks the lives of the unborn
matter than the women who carry them
perhaps one day you'll realize we weren't
toxic
you were—
i try to forgive and forget,
but i have a lot of anger for those who think
i should die
simply because i exist.
-linda m. crate

open up your eyes

it's dangerous sometimes to be who you truly are, but i would
rather be honest with myself than to live behind an ornamented
lie; no gilded cages will ever hold me—my wings were made to
fly, and i would rather be free for one moment than to live my life
on my knees begging for permission to exist; i am a match that is
ignited—there's no putting my fires out now that they've started, i
will burn your forest of nightmares until only light and truth can
shine through; i know you feel threatened by the existence of
people you don't understand but your anger is misplaced—we
were born how we were, we were never mistakes; we were
never the failures you wanted to make us out to be—we were just
born different, and different isn't always a terrible thing; open up
your mind and you might see the world has many hues and some
of them are very different than everything you've always known.
-linda m. crate

who are you to say?

you may lose respect for me when you find out my truth, but
that's okay; i've already lost some for you—i don't think you're
truly a bad person but a misguided one, one who thinks rules are
more important than love and compassion and understanding; and
i wish i could say that it's okay—but when people are persecuted
for who they are, when people are stoned to death and killed
simply because they love people they're "not supposed to" love it
makes me sick to my stomach and it is hard to breathe—it is
dizzying to me that some people would choose bigotry over
understanding, when i fell in love with a girl i was so disgusted and
i hated myself for the longest time; but my shame was taken
away from me—because you see there is nothing inherently evil
about love, but there is an evilness in judgment and in hatred and
justifying your hatred for another soul; we are all together on this
earth—we need to co-exist even if we do not always understand
another it doesn't mean we're both wrong or we're both right, we
both simply are; and isn't it beautiful that the world houses so
many different varieties of thoughts and peoples and cultures—
who are you to say i'm loving wrong?
-linda m. crate

mythology of my bones

you may hate me,
but the mythology of my bones
is one founded in love;
and i will never return the hate
you might make me angry or frustrated
but i will never attempt to wound you
the way you have me—
just because you don't understand something
doesn't make it wrong
just because you don't recognize someone
as a person doesn't mean they
don't exist or they shouldn't,
it just means
you don't fathom their meaning or truth;
but their truth doesn't become false
simply because you dislike them
or misunderstand them or misinterpret
what they have to say—
you are to love one another
so let each of us live our lives as we ought
loving as we ought
without judgment.
-linda m. crate

not your punching bags

always us vs. them mentality,
but why must there be victors and villains?
why can't we have conversations and connect
despite our differences?
why must it always be war?
don't you understand:
we *are* you,
looking for love and acceptance
we want a place in the world;
no one should say we don't belong
we do—
you use words as weapons,
but we were all made in God's image if you
want to argue theology with me;
so you have to accept that perhaps everything
you know as truth isn't the full truth
perhaps swallow your judgment because you aren't saints
waving your anger and hatred as weapons—
it's pretty sad when laws are put into place that ministers
accept our community all because you didn't have
the common sense to treat people like people
instead of punching bags.
-linda m. crate

my truth is mine

every dog likes bones,
but you won't
feast on mine;
i am not here to make you
feel better for the skeletons
hidden in your closet
nor to be your token—
i loved a woman once
lived a lifetime of shame for
all the crushes on women
i've had and the love i had for her,
but i am no longer ashamed;
no one has the right to tell me who to love
my heart falls regardless of your rules
for whomever it pleases—
i won't live in fear of your judgment
anymore
maybe it will cost me our friendship,
but if you cannot accept me for who i am
then your friendship is meaningless
to me anyway;
i am love and light
my truth may be different than yours
but that doesn't make it wrong.
-linda m. crate

i refuse to become the monster

you must ask me how i fell in love with a woman once, and i
cannot tell you that only why; she woke in me the magic in me i
thought long dead and gone when my heart had grown numb in
such a painful way i literally felt as if i were being torn in two—
when i had no faith in myself she had faith in me, she predicted
one day my books would be on the new york's time best seller list,
she bought me roses, she listened to me, she taught me my scars
made me beautiful, she did not shy away from the ugly parts of
me, she encouraged my writing and found worth in my words,
she never made me feel like a burden, we went on adventures like
dracula's ball and to see *the producers* and on walks in our
college town and campus, she made me feel everything all at once
and her faerie song reminded me of my own wings so that i could
fly again instead of struggling to run from all the foes who had
gotten comfortable with my broken pieces; and though she never
reciprocated my love i love her still—oceans of years part us, a
disagreement that was entirely my fault exploded into something it
should not have; and yet here she remains in my heart forever—a
place you may not have in my life, don't scoff, i have no time for
people committed to misunderstanding me; blood or not family are
the people who accept me as i am not the people who refuse—so
i fare thee well, stranger, if you cannot look at me with anything
but hate in your heart; i refuse to become the monster you'll
always be to me.
-linda m. crate

don't make your pain a weapon

i'm not dead yet
won't let you
bury me
you can throw your sticks and stones,
but you're not the only one
who can sharpen
their tongue or wit into a weapon;
be careful who you're judging because it might
just fall back on you—
you may have seen me fall,
but i will always rise;
tears may fall from my eyes
but i will always have this because i refuse
to let anyone define me but me—
i know those who talk behind my back
are already behind me,
but what ever happened to treating others
as you would wish to be treated?
i don't want drama
just want to live my life without negativity,
and i will cut out anyone
who doesn't let me live my dreams;
because who is anyone to tell another soul
who they are or how to live?
none of us is perfect,
but that is no reason to be cruel;
i don't use my pain as a weapon against you
so don't use yours as a weapon against me.
-linda m. crate

& we are all beautiful

didn't think i was lgbtq enough to share
my stories and my pain,
but i realize now more than ever
it is important;
someone might hear and realize
to open up their eyes
because truth doesn't always come in the form
of some great epiphany—
sometimes it comes in the form of a song,
or a poem or a book;
sometimes it comes in the form of someone
unapologetically being themselves
and if i can help one person in this universe
to love themselves
in a world where they couldn't before
then i have succeeded
because every heart is a treasure
even if they never receive the care and love they deserve
we are all made in the image of the universe—
& we are all beautiful
just the way we are.
-linda m. crate

clean that tongue of yours

your heart need not be a weapon yet you fan
the flames of discord,
somehow you think your voice is more
important than mine
or theirs;

we're just trying to live
to be proud of who we are
in a world that often condemns us
telling us we're mistakes—

you weren't born a bigot,
but somewhere along the lines
you lost your compassion;

only have it for you and yours
if yours happen to be like you otherwise no—

but i must have missed the verse
that said hate your sons and daughters
or hurt your neighbor as you'd hurt yourself

i must have missed the verse
that gave you authority to judge others,
and you say God doesn't like ugly?
well, stop being ugly then;
clean that tongue of yours that struggles
to be a weapon of love or truth but just an
instrument of chaos casting more
nightmares into this world.
-linda m. crate

please love me, too

guess i put my faith
in the wrong person

expected you to be my hero,
but i am my own;
i don't need your sword
slay my own monsters

i wear a crown of moonlight
and flowers;
i wear a thousand years of rage and pain
on my fevered fury
i use it to slash through the darkness
of nightmares—

it's okay
when the dust settles
i hope that we can still love one another
that we can still be friends

because i am still the same person i always was,
don't be scared;

things always change and sometimes people
change too
but i will always love you
please love me, too.
-linda m. crate

things don't have to be this way, you know?

you can preach your intolerance and your hate,
but i am the white winged valkryie of love and light
i will shatter your wrath with my dreams and my hopes;

you may think you are doing the right thing
but hate is never the right choice
anger rarely solves problems, either, and violence
certainly doesn't;

but sometimes we have to fight wars we don't want
simply because there is a time for peace and a time for
war—

you want to condemn, you want to judge, you
want to throw stones;

but i see your sins and i do not hold them against you
i see your lies and i do not undo you
because if you are so committed to undoing yourself then
i will let you make a mockery of yourself—

things don't have to be this way, you know?
you could preach love, you could preach compassion,
and you could admit sometimes there are things you don't
know the answers to

instead of insisting someone's very existence is wrong.
-linda m. crate

you just hate anyone different

all this month
i have seen your hatred
explode from
your fingertips,
i have seen your judgment
and your condemnation;
i have said nothing
but i have no less pride in myself
simply because you see no
worth in my existence—
you've shown your true colors
without knowing mine,
but the land mines of your words
may one day explode in your face
so maybe then you'll see
that hate is never the answer;
you don't have to understand someone
to respect them
yet you don't even have the decency to do
that—
hope no one in your family ever comes out
you'd probably cut them off
for something they couldn't even control,
something that's not even their fault;
i am sickened and repulsed
by the things you've said about this community
under the guise of religion
because the truth is you just hate anyone
who isn't the same as you.
-linda m. crate

i am worth it

won't relinquish my power, won't relinquish my love, won't beg
you for anything; i will ask for mercy and understanding but i think
your heart is set on war—if it is a battle you want, go ahead and
throw all the shade you want; you can't pray the gay away nor
can you wit it away so feel free to rip into me because i am strong
enough to take it—all my life i have been mocked and bullied for
one reason or another, but if i weren't special then none of these
people would keep trying to break me; and so i stand tall and
proud—rainbows are formed when prisms of light are met with
water and i have cried enough storms into existence to know that i
should not be shamed for myself, and i won't be; if you can't take
the lightening and the thunder then you don't deserve to see the
full spectrum of all my colors—i am full of red autumn leaves,
orange laughter, yellow daffodils, green grasses, blue moons,
indigo stars, and violet rivers of night—i don't expect you to
understand, but hope you realize you're the real loser here if you
choose to lose me; because i am worth it—always have been,
always will be.
-linda m. crate

my heart is full of love

i am sick of running, sick of living in fear, sick of worrying over
who will love me if they know the truth; i am done hiding all of my
power, all my magic, all my strength; i am a goddess full of divinity
and light—the only thing i'm going to chase are my dreams—and
i'm sorry if my identity confuses you or makes you question
yourself but that's not my problem, i am who i am; and you don't
get an 'a' for effort just for sticking around if you are going to ask
me who i love—just because i loved a woman once doesn't mean
i only fall in love with women or that i am attracted to all women,
you don't need to hide your wives and sisters; you don't need to
vilify me to justify an excuse to hide from me—my pan won't rub
off on you, it's not contagious; but if you stick around you might
just believe in yourself at such a frequency that you chase the
ugly things away because my heart is full of one thing: love.
-linda m. crate

on your furious forehead

you won't make me straight
have been with many men
that simply make me repulsed

at how thoughtless and insincere
some of them can be,
i think only one of them ever

loved me back but i cannot be sure
because we don't talk anymore;
all the others seemed interested in one

thing and one thing alone—
you don't own a woman,
and we are not your property;

yet if your masculinity is challenged
by the fact that sometimes i have girl
crushes and once i loved a woman

i cannot help the fact you are so fragile;
walked too many years on eggshells trying not to break eggs
you can fry them on your furious forehead if you need to.
-linda m. crate

when you choose to understand

i have a worth
even if you cannot see it,
and i don't really care
if you don't understand who i am;
have never tried to hurt
someone
just because they didn't see things
from my point of view—
sometimes pain can make you wound
others unintentionally,
but don't take it out on me;
it's not my fault
you cannot comprehend someone
that isn't like you—
i was taught empathy, compassion, and love;
so these are the things i choose
the tools i wield against my enemies are only
weapons that the darkness of nightmares and monsters fear—
i don't wish to hurt anyone,
but i know sometimes i must even if unintentionally;
i do know one thing
blowing out my candle doesn't make yours
shine brighter so let me hold onto this light of mine and maybe
i will light your candle one day
when you choose to understand.
-linda m. crate

reclaiming my kingdom

you'll believe in
miracles,
but you won't believe
in me;
and that's probably
the most painful thing—
you'll look for that little touch
of heavenly light elsewhere,
but you will try to dig up the dirt on me;
i have a history
we all do
i wasn't always the victim nor was i always
the villain
just some shade between
as most of us are—
but i am not ashamed of love
once i loved a girl,
but that doesn't make me less
of a person, a daughter, or a friend;
it doesn't make me less
of a magical or divine creature
the truth is if my power weren't so great
you wouldn't be sitting there trying to break it—
only difference is now i'm grown i'm not
going to kiss the feet of the people who kick me,
i'm going to pull them off their imaginary thrones
and reclaim my kingdom.
-linda m. crate

you're the wrong type of person

i have always been the right woman
not going to listen
if you tell me that i'm wrong

think i know my heart
better than you ever will
try walking a mile in my heels

i bet your legs would break
so don't act as if you can do anything
i have accomplished

you are you and i am me,
and i am glad that's the way things are;
because i couldn't live with myself

if i were a bigot
you say that my community is corrupt
but there's corruption in yours—

it is staring you straight in the face,
but i guess you don't think lives matter
unless they're cis and white and submissive;

letting their rights be stomped on
and their country be lead into a rapid death
i am not going to let the vultures devour us—

so you may think i'm the wrong specimen,
but i think you're the wrong type of person;
you favor rules over people and that's just gross.
-linda m. crate

we write our own stories

i think you need to relax and unpack your issues with the lgbtq
community, because you're harmful to everyone in the statements
you make; i don't know why we are your targets—but i am tired
of it, every day you've made a statement about the community
that i cannot ignore, don't say anything but i am well aware;
thought maybe your outrage would simmer and fizzle out but you
still seem to want to spit in the face of anyone who isn't
straight—listen, i know you think what you're doing is right, but
love isn't hate and your anger isn't helping anyone not even
yourself; i think you need to take a few seats and recognize that
there's more to this than you understand—you see us all as
monsters, but you're the one with the teeth and the claws tearing
us apart; can't blame us for not sitting there like lambs for the
slaughter—we've got to defend ourselves by any means we have
at our disposal, we won't be your victims nor your villains—we
write our own stories just as you do yours.
-linda m. crate

you don't need to plant landmines

i've been rejected all my life
for various reasons
by people i held respect for,
and i guess that's why
your bigotry in this matter
stings me so hard;
you are the wasp
coming after me simply
for existing—
like every other wasp
who has hunted me, however,
i will knock you to the ground and smash
you beneath my feet;
i will not be stomped out existence
simply because you cannot wrap your mind
around fathoming the truth of someone
who walks a different path than you—
you must walk your truth,
and i must walk mine;
but you do not need to plant landmines
in my life
hoping that i'll explode simply because
you lack empathy or compassion.
-linda m. crate

but bigotry is

it hurts
because if it were you
i wouldn't let you
feel shame,
i wouldn't wound you;
wouldn't forsake you
leaving you to linger in your pain
and self-doubt
wondering if you deserve to exist
after all—
i will not give you that power over me
all my life i have been hesitant
to be my authentic self
for fear of stepping on toes or making waves,
but i am the daughter of the moon;
i was born to make waves
refuse to wrap my arms around port any longer
i will embark on this voyage in the waters—
not everyone will understand,
but i am done hating myself for something
i can't even control;
love is never anything to be ashamed of
but bigotry is.
-linda m. crate

stop dividing and conquering

i understand you may not agree
you say the lifestyle is wrong,
but people are out there
just trying to live their lives;
they don't need your approval to exist
but a little kindness and empathy can go
a long way—
we all have room to improve
each of us is flawed,
but if we support each other instead of looking
to divide and conquer;
perhaps we'd be able to make this world
a better place—
doesn't need to be an us vs. them
mentality,
not everything needs to be a war;
just live and let live
many things in the universe exist without me understanding them
yet i don't condemn them for living their lives
such is the same
you don't have to understand but you can accept
a person for who they are
without judgment.
-linda m. crate

& i won't be sorry for who i am

i have to be brave in a world which sometimes scares me, i have
to hold my head up high when sometimes i feel i have no more
strength left to give; and i have seen the vultures circling—people
are all too happy to tell you when you're wrong or how you've
screwed up, but no one is there to comfort you in your need; no
one is there to whisper all the reassurances you need to be built
up but they're more than happy to tear you down—it is why i
have never broached the subject before now, but i know that i
must face who i am; i am not scared and i am not ashamed of my
identity because i know i am more than these flesh and bones—
my soul isn't sullied or bad because my path is different than
yours, my heart is full of love and light; i cannot help who i love
and i will not feel disgraced or discouraged because of that—i
know there are things beyond my understanding, and perhaps this
is one of them; but if i have survived uncertainty and failure
before then i will rise again from the ashes until i get it right—
refuse to believe myself lesser, refuse to surrender my power, i
was made beautifully in the image of the creator; so you cannot
tell me i am only my flaws—i am so much more than the broken
things you focus on seeing, i am so much more than your condem-
nation; i am a valkyrie warrior full of love and light whose halo
sings in rainbows—if you don't like that, well, i'm sorry; but no
one likes everything about you—& i won't be sorry for who i am.
-linda m. crate

won't let the asteroids of judgment make me hide

i have struggled to accept myself on so many levels,
and this one is another
i have wrestled with for many moons;
but i know that love is nothing to be shamed of—
i won't let you cheapen my identity
because of one faucet of my personality
i am a woman of many sinks, tubs, oceans, creeks,
rivers, streams, and skies full of rain;
i won't let you tell me i have no power
my voice is my weapon of choice
all my life my heart has known nothing but war
every day i was always reminded of how different
i was from everyone else
called weird by even family and friends
i don't see it as an insult now—
none of us is perfect,
but i try my best to be the best version of me;
so i refuse to paint myself into the darkness i am going to open
up every sunset and let her rainbow sing
regardless of whom it may offend—
i am done hiding out of fear
going to let my ship ride it out even on the rockiest of journeys
through space because i cannot let the asteroids of judgment hide
my
cosmic fires and my stars of radiant dreams and love.
-linda m. crate

i pray for better tomorrows

you would crucify me
simply for existing
my heart is full of love,
but you would insist
i deserve this;
you wouldn't want me
as your moral compass because
you'd insist i was tainted in some way—
but maybe it's you whose
mind is full of twisted nightmares
all i've ever wanted to do was make
the world a better place,
and all you do is spew hate and anger
in a world already riddled with
far too much of it;
maybe you're not so full of courage as you believe
if someone like me can scare you—
you can judge me if you have no better pastimes,
but i am going to live my life
doing the best i can
for myself and everyone else;
you and i are different—
i pray for better tomorrows, that you have eyes
that can discern truth;
you pray for the end of the world and for me to fall.
-linda m. crate

wouldn't spend a moment in your bones

there is a music in my soul i cannot silence
done pretending that hiding in this closet was ever comfortable,
and i won't thread a narrative of lies to make myself
better than who i truly am;
i know that i am far from perfect but we're all flawed—

maybe stop pointing fingers
i know your anger stems from a fear of what you don't know
that your hatred isn't founded in any figment of reality,
but of all the possibilities you don't want to be true;
you bend me out of shape make me a nightmare and a shade of
villain

so you can say your hands are clean
when you try to murder my identity and silence my voice—

but you'd still be a murderer
so don't ever think your hands are clean
when you are choking the life
of people who simply want to be accepted as they are
my sexuality isn't the only part of me that exists,

and if to be right
it means that i have to be cruel and crucify innocence
to bloat my ego then i would rather be myself
in every universe
than to be a moment in your bones.
-linda m. crate

i have a heart full of love

i know some people might hate me for who i am, but i cannot be anything less than me; i am who i am ever changing and evolving—i am unlearning years of wrong things well intentioned so i can embrace myself more freely, i refuse to wear the corset society tries to tie around my waist; won't be choked of who i am and become only a mother and a wife without an identity of my own—i won't forgo my dreams or stop chasing rainbows because there is the magic of a zillion or more universes in my veins, cannot you not hear all my planets and all my stars calling out to you for understanding? i only want peace in a life where i have always been warring against myself and others—i prefer compassion and flowers, but if i must, if i must; then i will ride out in the chariots of war and i will fight for my right to existence—i refuse to surrender to suffering and abuse, i have a heart full of love, i should not be faulted for that.

-linda m. crate

my love is a love unconditional

you don't see your ugliness
when you spew hatred,
but i see your anger;
why do you thrive on seeing
my pain?
what is it about my tears that makes
you feel like heaven is breathing
her gentle kiss upon your lips?
i am done kneeling in supplication
because you are not gods,
and your praise and your rejection
equally mean nothing to me
because you are cruel and condemning;
you prefer laws that kill people
rather than to simply hold your arms out
helping them to the love you say
you truly are—
i am done being insulted by you
because you should have no power over me,
and your words are just words
of angry men;
people who don't understand are often loud
about their disapproval
you can disapprove as much as you want
it won't change the fact that my love is a love
unconditional falling for souls not bodies.
-linda m. crate

because my place is here

summer is blooming
every pretty flower
beating to the breath
of sunlight snaking
against the grasses and laughing
through the trees,

but you are winter;
deadly and cruel and whispering
of condemnation and demanding reflection
when i've already considered
the reasons to hate myself—

& i don't want to think about all my flaws
we all have them,
and i am trying my best in spite of them
to be the best person i can be;

i am not afraid of your castles of glass
your rocks will ricochet
breaking you of your home,
opening in you all the wounds you cast
upon others;
maybe it will be only then that you see

your hatred was unfounded
when you could have sewn shut wounds
instead of opening them wide in other hearts—

but i can't hide in a closet
when i see all these beautiful rainbows summer has
to sing into existence,
i cannot hug skeletons when i know they make
poor conversationalists;
so i am done letting you put me in my place

because my place is here
as i am.
-linda m. crate

different lenses and laughters and loves

guess you love
oppressing others

maybe it keeps your mind
off your own oppression
how you forsook love to grasp
onto harpoons of hatred,

you work the same system
as many of us are forced to;

cogs in a machine
designed to crush us all
yet you take pride in it
as if being a ghost without a name
inhaled by void is something
to be proud of—

but i am sorry i cannot be *that* person
some crave simplicity,
but i have always loved all the varieties
of art in the world and in my imagination;
so many different veins and bloods and skeins
of magic wrapping tendrils
like ivy around trees—

we are all different
maybe just embrace that we all
have different lenses and laughters and loves,

and accept that none of us is wrong
because love is the only magic that can save us all.
-linda m. crate

i'm certain you are

you want to force your path
upon the shoulders
of others
forgetting you were given the option
of choosing
so let them see who you truly are
let go of all your hate and rage
if you are love then let us see it,
because your bigotry
makes me feel physically ill;
i loved a woman once and sometimes
get crushes on girls
sometimes a sea gull sits on the pier
and sometimes she flies
just a natural thing—
yet you would act is if i were sick
or one the ledge of ruin,
and if you throw me overboard
i will just swim;
because i am a daughter of the moon
the ocean has never been my enemy
but you,
i'm certain you are.
-linda m. crate

rainbow soul and all

i live in a world
which sometimes makes
little sense to me,
which always misunderstands who
i truly am;
misfit truly
anywhere i am
it is hard to be comfortable in my own skin
at times—
but i know who i am,
and i will not regret her
even if you do;
i may not be the smartest or the prettiest
or the bravest
but i am me doing the best i can
always—
i have learned to love myself
jagged edges and all
rainbows
have always been my favorite thing,
as if the universe were trying to nudge me all along
in the right direction;
but after years of denying who i was
to make everyone else happy
i am proud to stand in my own skin
rainbow soul and all.
-linda m. crate

the dreaming she woke in me

spent my whole life
trying not to
disturb the peace,
walking on egg shells
until i was so numb
that nothing could move me;
and then she woke what slept so
deeply within: the dreaming—
so, you see,
i don't regret loving her at all
even if it confused me then;
and i am sorry if this makes me
less worthy of their love
but you can walk away
so many people died to me
whilst they were still alive
chose to leave me quilted in a silence
i didn't understand—
so believe me when i say i will see you walking,
but i won't try to make you stay;
if you cannot love me as i am then don't love me at all
because conditional love isn't something i want.
-linda m. crate

little earthquakes

of words
shake everything up

i am trying to seek
a firm foundation within myself
that you shouldn't challenge
who i am

so what if i am not like you?

that's no reason to hate someone.

if your religion tells you
to hate someone
i can promise you that you're
practicing wrong

because religions are supposed
to be about relationships with yourselves
and your gods—

they require no judgment,
and they require no hatred and anger;

i am sewing up my tectonic plates
so the volcanoes don't erupt all those painful ashes
into the universe
i refuse to be the monsters you were to me;
although my inner vampire thirsts for blood
i will hold onto peace, for now.
-linda m. crate

heart full of love

i was given my name and my life
that's all the universe set into motion

my choices and my indecisions
brought me here,
now i am more sure of myself

i am grown;
but even still my feet look for firm footing
when i am crawling down the banks
of life

don't want to fall into some creek
not meant for me—

so many twisted roots and trees
overlooked,
but i have always found beauty in strange things

perhaps this is why i have always
been caged in bones and verses people claim
eccentric, odd, weird;

but i would rather have a heart full of love
than be a bigot full of religion.
-linda m. crate

my heart won't be poisoned

denied myself
too many years

people saw me as a
doormat,
walking over me;

but i am not some pushover
simply because i am kind hearted
and well intentioned—

i am a warrior of love and light
fighting for her place in the world

my truth may be different than yours,
but that doesn't make either of us
liars;

it just means you are you and i am me—

stop trying to force me into
your box because i don't even fit into
my own let alone know where it's located,

let us agree to disagree;
we can be respectful
despite our differences

my heart won't be poisoned
by your heart or fear.
-linda m. crate

mean bird, fly away

you are a blue jay
trying to push me away,
but i don't care;

i am a phoenix
full of love and light
always rising from the ashes
of every death to rise
again—

mean bird,
you won't force me to be
anyone else;

i can only be me
everyone else is already taken—

mean bird,
you aren't right simply because
of your insistence;

you may have fists
i have a soul

so what if i've loved a girl?
in the end what does that do to you,
nothing?

perhaps leave it alone then.
-linda m. crate

so now i will sing

sometimes the world can be a scary place just to exist in, regardless, of who you are; but i refuse to be afraid of myself or my truth—if *harry potter* taught you anything it should be that no one should have to live in a closet, and should you think yours is cleaned of skeletons go ahead and think again; because we both know no one is perfect—yet you would hold me to that unattainable standard with your judgment, and i don't even know what to do with all your rage because i have fury of my own; all i know is i have is the right to exist—i hear my voice, and she tells me to keep going no matter what; so even if my truth forces you to reject me i am going to be who i am—i have dreams to chase and catch and make mine, i am done remaining silent about who i truly am simply to keep others happy; i have spent too many years in quiet so now i will sing.

-linda m. crate

www.ingramcontent.com/pod-product-compliance
Lightning Source LLC
Chambersburg PA
CBHW060448160726
47992CB00003B/1126